Life After the American Revolution

Linda R. Wade

ABDO
& Daughters

Visit us at
www.abdopub.com

Published by ABDO Publishing Company, 4940 Viking Drive, Edina, MN 55435.
Copyright ©2001 by Abdo Consulting Group, Inc. International copyrights
reserved in all countries. No part of this book may be reproduced in any form
without written permission from the publisher.

Printed in the United States.

Contributing Editor, Graphic Design, Illustrations: John Hamilton
Cover photo: Corbis
Interior photos: John Hamilton, p. 1, 11, 15, 31
Corbis, p. 4, 7, 8, 17, 21, 23, 25, 27
Independence National Historical Park, p. 13, 14

Sources: Collins, Robert A. *The History of America.* New York: CLB
Publishing, 1993; Gay, Kathlyn. *Revolutionary War.* New York: Twenty-First
Century Books, A Division of Henry Holt and Company, Inc., 1995; Grant, R.
G. *The American Revolution.* New York: Thomas Learning, 1995; Kent,
Deborah. *America the Beautiful: (*series*).* Chicago: Childrens Press, 1988;
Microsoft Encarta '97 Encylopedia; Stewart, Gail. *The Revolutionary War.* San
Diego: Lucent Books, 1991; Stine, R. Conrad. *America the Beautiful: New
York: New York.* Chicago: Children's Press, 1989.

Library of Congress Cataloging–in–Publication Data

Wade, Linda R.
   Life after the American Revolution / Linda R. Wade
      p. cm. -- (The American Revolution)
   Includes index.
   ISBN 1-57765-079-4
   1. United States--History--Revolution, 1775-1783--Peace--Juvenile literature. 2.
United States--History--Revolution, 1775-1783--Casualties--Juvenile literature. [1.
United States--History--Revolution, 1775-1783--Peace] I. Title.

   E249 .W22 2001
   973.3'16--dc21

                                              00-049601

CONTENTS

INTRODUCTION

On October 19, 1781, the Liberty Bell rang out loud and clear. British soldiers surrendered their guns at Yorktown. The war would not officially be over for two more years. Still, this was a day to celebrate.

The Liberty Bell ringing in celebration in Philadelphia, Pennsylvania.

What began as 13 colonies became the United States of America. For eight years these colonies struggled for independence. In many cases family members fought each other. Some had remained true to Great Britain. Others defended the policies of independence long before Lexington and Concord.

America grew up during those eight years. The war changed the lives of everyone. Men who had never been more than two miles from their home had now walked many miles in several states. Women found that they could do more than take care of children and clean and cook.

The last few years of the eighteenth century are possibly the most important years in the history of the United States.

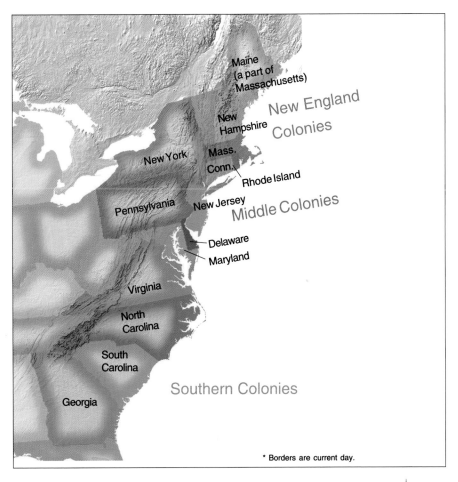

* Borders are current day.

CHAPTER 1

WHY DID THE AMERICANS WIN THE WAR?

It would seem that a powerful British army should have been able to squash the unprepared colonists. The British often had more men. They marched in proper position. They appeared to do everything right. Why was it, then, that the Americans won the war?

One reason was probably the fact that the British army was so far from home. All of their supplies had to be delivered by ship. The army had to stay near the sea to receive these shipments of supplies.

Another reason was that the Americans were fighting on their own soil. To lose the war meant that many of the patriots would be hanged for treason. The Americans were also fighting for liberty. Their homes were at stake. Their families were depending on them. Victory meant freedom. Defeat offered only an uncertain future.

The colonists were encouraged when other countries helped them. The Germans and French were especially helpful. Friedrich von Steuben organized and trained the army during the fateful winter at Valley Forge. The Frenchman Marquis de Lafayete brought soldiers from France and received important assignments from the Americans.

A lithograph of the fife and drum players of A.M. Willard's famous painting.

Leadership was also an important factor. The American leaders were respected and obeyed. General George Washington was their supreme commander. They knew he would not ask more than he was able to do himself. He understood his men. He did all he could to train them and make them successful soldiers.

As a result, the soldiers fought harder. They stayed on the lines when their feet were freezing. They endured the hardships of marching. Often they went hungry. They gave their best for their country.

The Americans' intense desire to win drove them from battle to battle. Even in the face of defeat, they never gave up.

American colonists and British soldiers fight at the top of Breed's Hill (Bunker Hill), in Boston, Massachusetts.

General Washington, as painted by Charles Wilson Peale.

CHAPTER 2

WAR LOSSES

Loss of life was high during the Revolutionary War, with fatalities totaling about 25,700 soldiers:

- 7,200 were killed in battle.
- 10,000 died in military camps, often from sickness.
- 8,500 died in prison after being captured.

Another 9,600 American soldiers were wounded or missing in action.

The British military suffered too. Nearly 10,000 British soldiers died many miles away from home.

Serving as a soldier was not a guarantee of payment. Many of the soldiers received little or no pay. Their return home meant starting all over.

For those soldiers who fought the entire war, there was a certificate giving them land in the west. However, many sold their certificates.

The war was hard on the states financially. It took until the early 1800's to pay the war debt.

By April 26, 1783, over 100,000 Loyalists returned to England. They left because they were afraid they would be mistreated. This was a great loss to the new country, but those people who remained in America were dedicated to freedom and independence. They knew the days ahead would be difficult but they had great determination.

Granary Burying Ground, in Boston, Massachusetts.

CHAPTER 3

ARTICLES OF CONFEDERATION

Before the Constitution became law a set of rules was developed. In 1781, the states accepted a plan for a central government. It was called the Articles of Confederation. They created a republic. Voters of each state elected leaders who chose representatives. These representatives met together as the Congress. Each state had only one vote. The Articles gave most powers of government to the states.

Congress had many limitations. At least nine of the 13 states had to agree when making a new law. The states had difficulty agreeing on nearly everything.

No state wanted to be under the rule of another. They took this further, saying that they did not want to be ruled by an individual. The states were afraid of giving one person too much authority, like a king. Instead, a committee of representatives kept the government running when Congress was not meeting.

There was no national court system. Congress acted as a court for settling disagreements between the states. This did not work because the states did not always obey Congress.

It wasn't long before problems developed. The Articles were too weak. The states were not united. They began to quarrel with each other. They disagreed on boundary lines.

ARTICLES

OF

CONFEDERATION AND PERPETUAL UNION,

BETWEEN THE STATES OF

NEW-HAMPSHIRE,	~~The Counties of New-Castle~~
MASSACHUSETTS-BAY,	~~Kent and Sussex on~~ DELAWARE,
RHODE-ISLAND, *providence plantations*	MARYLAND,
CONNECTICUT,	VIRGINIA,
NEW-YORK,	NORTH-CAROLINA,
NEW-JERSEY,	SOUTH-CAROLINA, AND
PENNSYLVANIA,	GEORGIA.

ART. I. THE ~~name~~ *stile* of this Confederacy shall be "THE UNITED STATES OF AMERICA."

II Each State Retain its sovereignty Freedom & Independance & every power Jurisdiction & right, which is not by this Confederation expressly delegated to the united States in Congress assembled

ART. II. The said States hereby severally enter into a firm league of friendship with each other, for their common defence, the security of their liberties, and their mutual and general welfare, binding themselves to assist each other against all force offered to or attacks made upon them or any of them, on account of religion, sovereignty, trade, or any other ~~pretence~~ whatever.

ART. III. Each State reserves to itself the sole and exclusive regulation and government of its internal police in all matters that shall not interfere with the articles of this Confederation.

ART. IV. No State, without the consent of the United States in Congress Assembled, shall send any Embassy to or receive any embassy from, or enter into any conference, agreement, alliance or treaty with any King, Prince or State; nor shall any person holding any office of profit or trust under the United States or any them, accept of any present, emolument, office or title of any kind whatever from any King, Prince or foreign State; nor shall the United States Assembled, or any of them, grant any title of nobility.

ART. V. No two or more States shall enter into any treaty, confederation or alliance whatever between them without the consent of the United States in Congress Assembled, specifying accurately the purposes for which the same is to be entered into, and how long it shall continue.

ART. VI. No State shall lay any imposts or duties which may interfere with any stipulations in treaties ~~hereafter~~ entered into by the United States Assembled with any King, Prince or State. *in pursuance of any Treaties, already proposed by Congress to the Courts of France & Spain*

Page one of the Articles of Confederation.

The states passed taxes on goods imported from neighboring states. New York had a tax on all farm produce from New Jersey. Connecticut taxed goods coming from Massachusetts. Such taxes discouraged trade between the states. Business owners and merchants disliked the taxes, but Congress had no power to get rid of them.

Congress could print paper money, but it printed too much. The result was inflation, with prices rising out of control. Congress had borrowed money to pay for war. This money had purchased food, clothing for the soldiers, as well as military equipment. It even owed the soldiers for their service. For three years Congress could not even pay the salaries of its own members. Creditors wanted to be paid.

It was obvious that changes had to be made in the government. But first, the Revolutionary War had to be totally settled.

John Dickinson of Delaware headed the committee that drafted the Articles of Confederation, the first "constitution" of the United States.

Taxes and tariffs made it difficult for merchants to trade from state to state.

CHAPTER 4

THE TREATY OF PARIS

In April 1782, peace discussions between the Americans and the British began in Paris. The British sent Richard Oswald to Paris to talk with Benjamin Franklin. The following terms were set to legally end the war:

• The British had to accept American independence and remove British soldiers from American soil.

• Franklin asked that the British pay for towns that they had destroyed during the war.

• The British asked that the Loyalists who remained in the United States be treated fairly.

• Americans were given fishing rights off the coast of Newfoundland and Nova Scotia.

On November 30, 1782, the Americans and British signed a preliminary peace treaty in Paris. The United States was named as a new nation.

On April 15, 1783, Congress ratified the preliminary peace treaty. Then, on September 3, 1783, the United States and Great Britain signed the final document. Congress ratified the Treaty of Paris on January 14, 1784. Thus, the Revolutionary War was officially over. At long last, 13 individual colonies had become one nation.

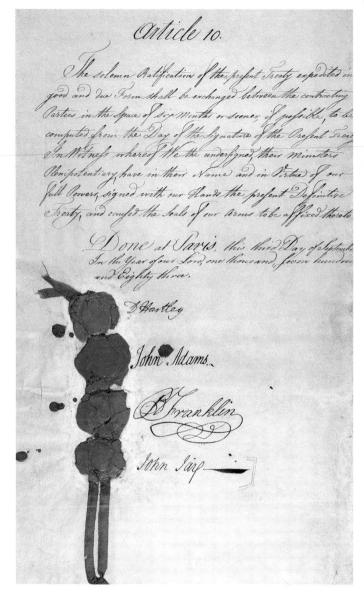

The 1783 Treaty of Paris, which ended the American Revolution and recognized the independence of the United States.

The borders of this new country went south to Florida. An imaginary line cut through the Great Lakes. The western border was the Mississippi River.

There were three million people in the 13 new states. Now they had to devise a plan to unite the country.

CHAPTER 5

PROBLEMS OF THE EARLY YEARS

The United States government did not suddenly happen. There were many growing pains over the next few years. Thomas Jefferson led a congressional committee that wanted to divide some of the western territories into states. He also proposed a ban on slavery everywhere in the United States after 1800. It failed to pass by a narrow margin.

Foreign countries were also changing politics. In August 1784, the United States began trading goods with China. The following month Russia established a settlement on Kodiak Island in Alaska.

John Adams became an ambassador to Great Britain in February 1785. He worked to settle problems with the British forts located along the Canadian border. The pre-war debts owed to British creditors as well as treatment of Loyalists were also topics of discussion. These problems were discussed but no solution was found.

The summer of 1786 brought problems for many Americans. There was a shortage of money, high taxes, pestering creditors, farm foreclosures, and bankruptcies. It was especially hard for farmers. People complained. They began talking about rebelling against the government.

Congress found some success with the Northwest Ordinance of 1787. The Northwest Territory was a huge area of land given up (ceded) by the British in 1783. Several states claimed the land as their own, but leaders in other states believed the new land should belong to the country, not the individual states.

The Northwest Ordinance was a plan, first devised by Thomas Jefferson, that allowed for the territories to become states. The ordinance guaranteed freedom of worship, public support of education, and freedom from slavery. Had Jefferson had his way, slavery in all the states would have been abolished after 1800, but his proposal was narrowly defeated.

The most important thing about the Northwest Ordinance was that it made it possible for new territories, instead of being treated like conquered lands, to become states equal with the original 13.

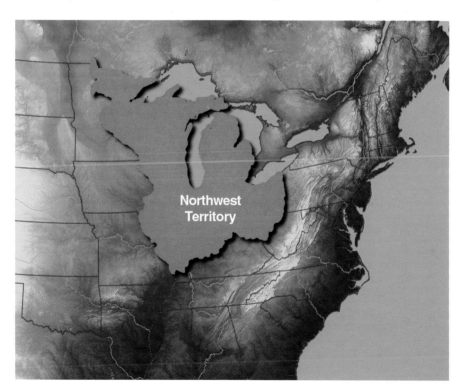

CHAPTER 6

SHAYS' REBELLION

For many people, positive actions like the Northwest Ordinance made little difference in their lives. Their problems were at home, not in the Northwest Territory.

Daniel Shays was one of many bankrupt farmers. Late in the summer of 1786, he gathered together representatives from 50 towns in Massachusetts. They discussed the situation, and then went into action. They marched to the courthouse in Northampton and kept it from holding a session. They approached the New Hampshire State Assembly and demanded a new issue of paper money.

By September, Shays' men were afraid they would be charged with treason. They headed for the Massachusetts Supreme Court in Springfield, and forced the court to adjourn.

Militiamen were called out, but seemed unable to stop the rebellion. But on February 4, 1787, General Benjamin Lincoln and his 4,400 men attacked Shays' rebels at Petersham, Massachusetts. Lincoln captured 150 men. Shays retreated to Vermont.

Shays' rebellion forced Congress to realize that the country needed a stronger central government. They endorsed a resolution calling for a constitutional convention to be held in Philadelphia beginning in May.

An engraving showing a brawl between a Massachusetts government supporter and a rebel, during Shays' Rebellion.

CHAPTER 7

WRITING THE UNITED STATES CONSTITUTION

James Madison was a young representative from Virginia. He was worried about the weaknesses of the Articles of Confederation. George Washington, Thomas Jefferson, and John Adams agreed with Madison. They encouraged state representatives to meet and try to solve some of the problems.

In 1787, Congress invited the states to a convention at Independence Hall in Philadelphia. George Washington arrived early and met with the Pennsylvania governor, 81-year-old Benjamin Franklin. His wisdom from years in governmental positions was helpful to Washington.

There were 55 delegates who came to the Constitutional Convention. They had planned to strengthen the Articles of Confederation. However, they soon realized that they needed to write a new constitution. To do this, they worked hard six days a week for four months. George Washington served as chairman of the convention.

James Madison had studied the government, and the leaders asked him to write the document. He took notes during the day and wrote them out at night.

James Madison, fourth president of the United States. Madison is known as the "master builder of the Constitution" for his part in drafting the document at the Constitutional Convention of 1787 in Philadelphia.

The new form of national government would be separated into three branches: the legislative, executive, and judicial.

The Legislative Branch is the Congress. It makes the laws for the United States. It is divided into two houses: the House of Representatives and the Senate.

The number of representatives each state sends to the House depends on the population of the state. That is one of the reasons a census is done. Representatives are elected every two years. It is possible for the number of representatives to change.

The Senate is different. Each state elects two senators every six years. In this way small states have an equal voice with the larger states.

The Executive Branch includes the president and cabinet. The president's main duties are to carry out the laws and head the armed forces.

The Judicial Branch includes the court system. The Supreme Court heads it. The president appoints the judges, but Congress must approve them. The Supreme Court has the power to decide whether laws are constitutional.

These three branches of government provide a system of checks and balances. Thus, no one branch has the final decision on matters that affect the people.

Here is how a proposal is made into a law: A proposal (bill) is made in either the House of Representatives or the Senate. After the bill passes that house it is sent to the other. If it passes the vote there, it is sent to the president. The president can sign or veto (reject) the bill. The Supreme Court rules on the laws of the land whenever there is a question.

George Washington watches from his desk as a delegate
signs the United States Constitution. Other delegates observe
the proceedings.

CHAPTER 8

THE CONSTITUTION BECOMES LAW

After the Constitution was written it had to be ratified (approved) by nine of the 13 states. One by one the state delegates approved this new form of government.

State	Date ratified
Delaware	December 7, 1787
Pennsylvania	December 12, 1787
New Jersey	December 18, 1787
Georgia	January 2, 1788
Connecticut	January 9, 1788
Massachusetts	February 6, 1788
Maryland	April 28, 1788
South Carolina	May 23, 1788
New Hampshire	June 21, 1788
Virginia	June 25, 1788
New York	July 26, 1788
North Carolina	November 21, 1789
Rhode Island	May 29, 1790

From January through June, 1788, people argued about the Constitution. They even went to the people in states that had not voted and tried to change their way of voting. Those who wanted the Constitution were called Federalists. Those who did not want it were known as Anti-Federalists.

The people were concerned that the Constitution did not mention individual rights. Finally, it was agreed that amendments would be added to the Constitution when it was approved. These amendments were called the Bill of Rights. Now the rights of individuals were also protected.

The Preamble to the United States Constitution. The original document is now displayed in the National Archives Building in Washington, D.C.

CHAPTER 9

THE NEW UNITED STATES

In 1789, George Washington became the first president of the United States. He went to New York and took the oath of office. John Adams was the vice president.

Two political parties began in Washington's first term of office. Thomas Jefferson and Alexander Hamilton argued over the government. Their differences formed these political parties. Jefferson felt that the country should continue to depend on agriculture. He was called a Republican. Hamilton said that the country should encourage manufacturing and the growth of cities. His party was called the Federalists.

There were many difficulties during those first few years. However, the leaders were determined. Their desire was to build a strong union. The Constitution endured those difficult years.

People now felt more secure. With the opening of the Northwest Territory, many wanted to reach out for land. They traveled over rough paths to make a new life for themselves and their families.

They were Americans. They were strong. They had overcome many problems. They had won their independence from Great Britain. Now it was time to move forward.

INTERNET SITES

ushistory.org
http://www.ushistory.org/

This Internet exploration of the Revolutionary War is presented by the Independence Hall Association. Visitors can learn interesting facts about many aspects of the war, including major battles, biographies of important patriots (Ben Franklin, Betsy Ross, Thomas Paine, and others), plus info on historic sites that can be toured today. The section on the Declaration of Independence includes photos of the document, as well as bios of the signers and Jefferson's account of the writing.

Liberty! The American Revolution
http://www.pbs.org/ktca/liberty/

The official online companion to "Liberty! The American Revolution," a series of documentaries originally broadcast on PBS in 1997. Includes timelines, resource material, and related topics—a potpourri of information on the American Revolution. Topics cover daily life in the colonies, the global village, a military point of view, plus a section on the making of the TV series. Also includes a "Revolutionary Game."

These sites are subject to change. Go to your favorite search engine and type in "American Revolution" for more sites.

PASS IT ON

American Revolutionary War buffs: educate readers around the country by passing on interesting information you've learned about the American Revolution. Maybe your family visited a famous Revolutionary War battle site, or you've taken part in a reenactment. Who's your favorite historical figure from the Revolutionary War? We want to hear from you!

To get posted on the ABDO Publishing Company Web site, email us at "History@abdopub.com"

Visit the ABDO Publishing Company Web site at www.abdopub.com

GLOSSARY

Ambassador

A person sent by a government to represent it in another country.

Anti-Federalists

People who did not want a strong national government.

Bill of Rights

The first 10 amendments to the U.S. Constitution.

Census

A population count of the people. It is taken every 10 years in the United States.

Compromise

To reach an agreement, usually by each side giving up something that the other wants.

Continental Army

The American army, led by George Washington.

Democracy

Rule of the people.

Federalists

People who wanted a strong national government.

Inflation

When money loses its face value, which results in goods costing more.

Loyalist

A person living in the colonies who remained true to Great Britain. They were also called Tories.

Ratify

To agree or to officially approve.

Republic

A form of government in which people elect representatives to run the country.

Treaty

An agreement between countries.

Veto

A refusal to sign a bill, which keeps it from becoming a law.

Philadelphia's Independence Hall.

INDEX